STEP-BY-STEP

15-Minute
Vegetarian

STEP-BY-STEP

15-Minute Vegetarian

Matthew Drennan

Photography by Amanda Heywood

To Mark and my parents, Jim and Betty, with thanks.

This edition published in 1996 by Smithmark Publishers,
a division of U.S. Media Holdings, Inc.,
16 East 32nd Street, New York NY 10016

SMITHMARK books are available for bulk purchase for sales promotion
and premium use. For details write or call the manager of special sales,
SMITHMARK Publishers
16 East 32nd Street
New York NY 10016
(212) 532-6600

© 1996 Anness Publishing Limited

ISBN 0-8317-7285-9

Publisher: Joanna Lorenz
Senior Cookery Editor: Linda Fraser
In-house Editor: Jillian Stewart
Designer: Alan Marshall
Photographer: Amanda Heywood
Home Economist: Stephen Wheeler
assisted by Lucy McKelvie

Printed and bound in Hong Kong

10 9 8 7 6 5 4 3 2 1

CONTENTS

INTRODUCTION

Vegetarian food has finally become a major part of our cuisine. We no longer need to justify the inclusion of vegetarian dishes on restaurant menus, and a cookbook such as this one reaches a wide audience, as more and more people become interested in a vegetarian menu. The notion that vegetarian dishes are uninspired, heavy and dull has long been dispelled, but one myth that does persist is the idea that vegetarian food is fussy and time-consuming. Fast food has become an important part of our culture. The demand for "real food" in this area is increasing, and vegetarian food is no exception.

Step-by-Step 15-Minute Vegetarian proves how easy it can be to produce a delicious vegetarian lunch or dinner in less time than it takes to reheat a ready-made meal from the supermarket. The emphasis is on freshly prepared produce cleverly coupled with staples from pantry or freezer.

The secret of success when speed is essential is to make sure you have all the ingredients and necessary equipment before you begin. Advice on stocking the pantry and what constitutes a survival kitchen is given on the next few pages. For quick cooking, cut ingredients to a similar size, and remember that root vegetables will take longer than most greens. Master the "all hands on deck" method, using the time while one item is cooking to prepare the next, and you may be surprised to discover just how speedy a cook you can be.

So whether you are a committed vegetarian, enjoy the occasional vegetarian meal, or just want something simple and satisfying because you are in a hurry or too tired to spend hours in the kitchen, this book brings you the means of making fantastic home-cooked meals in minutes.

The Pantry

Your pantry should be the backbone of your kitchen. Stock it sensibly, and you'll always have the means to make a tasty, satisfying meal. Begin with the basics and expand as you experiment, buying small quantities whenever possible and keeping an eye on "sell by" dates.

OILS, SAUCES AND CANNED GOODS

Chili oil
Use this fiery oil sparingly to liven up vegetable stir-fries and similar dishes.

Olive oil
If you must have only one oil, a good olive oil will suit most purposes (except deep-frying). Extra virgin olive oil is more expensive and best kept for salads.

Peanut oil
This bland-tasting oil will not mask delicate flavors. It is good for deep-frying. Use vegetable or sunflower oil instead, if you prefer.

Sesame oil
Favored in oriental cooking for its flavor, this rich oil can be used on its own or combined with vegetable oil.

Ghee
This is pure clarified butter used in Indian cooking. Make your own or substitute vegetable, corn or nut oil.

Black bean sauce
A thick aromatic sauce made from beans, used for marinades and stir-fries.

Passata/Strained tomatoes
This is a thick sauce made from strained tomatoes, used mainly in Italian cooking.

Soy sauce
A thin, salty, black liquid made from fermented soy beans. Add a splash at the end of cooking and offer extra at the table.

Sun-dried tomatoes
These deliciously sweet tomatoes, baked in the sun and dried, are sold in bags or in jars, steeped in olive oil.

Tahini
Made from ground sesame seeds, this paste is used in Middle Eastern cookery.

Tomato paste
This is a concentrated tomato sauce which is sold in cans, jars or tubes. A version made from sun-dried tomatoes is also now available.

Canned beans, lentils, peas
Chick-peas, cannellini beans, green lentils, haricot beans and red kidney beans survive the canning process well. Wash in cold running water, and drain well before use.

Canned vegetables
Although fresh vegetables are best for most cooking, some canned products are very useful. Artichoke hearts have a mild sweet flavor and are great for adding to stir-fries, salads or risottos. Pimientos are whole red bell peppers in jars, seeded and peeled. Use them for stews and soups, but stick to fresh bell peppers for anything else as they lack the firmness of bite that is needed for dishes such as stir-fries. Canned tomatoes are an essential ingredient to have in the pantry. There is now a very wide range available, whole or chopped, plain or with herbs, spices or other flavorings. Additional useful items to include are corn kernels, or ratatouille (found in specialty stores in jars, or at deli counters).

chick-peas

tahini

tomato paste

maple syrup

red wine

chili sauce

chopped
tomatoes

chili
oil

herb vinegar

pimientos

corn

white wine
vinegar

black olive
paste

ratatouille

kidney beans

lentils

soy sauce

black bean
sauce

tabini

plum tomatoes

chiles in oil

olive
oil

mustard

honey

strained
tomatoes

peanut
oil

red wine
vinegar

balsamic
vinegar

ghee

salad dressing

black olives

Dry Goods

Assuming your pantry already includes flours, sugars and dried fruits, the following items are invaluable for speedy cooking. The list of spices relates specifically to the recipes in this book.

Bulgur
This whole wheat grain is steam-dried and cracked before sale, so only needs a brief soaking before use. Keep it cool and dry in the pantry and it will last for a few months.

Nuts
Buy nuts in small quantities and store in a dry place. Almonds, cashews, peanuts, pecans, pine nuts and walnuts all feature prominently in this book.

Pasta
While fresh pasta is generally preferred, both for flavor and for speed of cooking, the dried product is a very valuable pantry ingredient. Spaghetti, noodles (Italian and oriental) and shapes are all useful.

Rice
If you stock only one type of rice, make it basmati, which has a superior flavor and fragrance. A mixture of basmati and wild rice (not a true rice, but the seeds of an aquatic grass) works well.

SPICES

Caraway seeds
Small greenish-brown seeds with a nutty texture and a flavor reminiscent of anise or fennel.

Chinese five-spice powder
Made from a mixture of anise pepper, cassia, fennel seed, star anise and cloves, this spice has an enticing anise (licorice) flavor.

Garam masala
This is an aromatic mixture of different spices used widely in Indian dishes. It is usually added at the end of cooking.

Ground cardamom
Fragrant, with a spicy undertone, cardamom is used in sweet and savory dishes.

Ground coriander
With a warm savory aroma, this spice imparts a mildly hot yet sweetish flavor.

Ground cinnamon
A sweet, fragrant spice ground from the dried rolled inner bark of a tropical tree.

Ground cumin
Sweet and pungent, with a unique and distinctive taste.

Ground turmeric
With a somewhat musty flavor and aroma, this spice adds a deep yellow color to food. It is sometimes used in place of saffron to add color, although it does not have the same flavor.

Saffron
This is the most expensive spice in the world. It has a pungent scent with a slightly bittersweet taste. The threads are crushed and steeped in a little liquid before use.

rice

ground turmeric

ground cumin

caraway

egg noodles

nuts

penne

bulgur

pecan nuts

garam
masala

dried chilies

spaghetti

cornstarch

mixed spice

black
peppercorns

Chinese five-
spice powder

pine nuts

poppy seeds

chili
powder

ground
coriander

sea salt

thyme

cumin seed

long grain
rice

granulated
sugar

garlic

Fresh Produce

Beautifully fresh herbs and vegetables from around the world are readily available in our supermarkets. This vegetable checklist highlights both familiar and less well-known items.

HERBS

Basil
Well known for its affinity with tomatoes, basil has a rich, spicy aroma.

Cilantro
A pungent, slightly sweet herb, commonly used in Indian cooking.

Oregano
This herb has a strong flavor. It is widely used in Italian cooking.

VEGETABLES

Chilies, red or green
Members of the capsicum (pepper) family, these are small and can be very fiery. Take care when handling chilies not to touch your eyes and mouth, as chilies contain an irritant which can sting sensitive skin.

Eggplant
A glossy oval or round vegetable, usually purple, eggplant is delicious broiled, fried or stuffed.

Fennel
A bulbous leaf stalk with a distinct anise flavor. Fennel can be eaten raw in salads, or cooked.

Shallots
These small bulbs have a mild onion flavor and are ideal for using in sauces.

Shiitake mushrooms
An oriental mushroom with a fairly meaty scent and flavor. The stems are quite tough and are best discarded.

Cheeses and Tofu

Improvements in handling and distribution mean that we are now able to buy a huge range of local and imported cheeses in excellent condition. Tofu, available in various forms, is another valuable source of protein.

Blue cheese
Where a recipe fails to specify a particular blue cheese, use Roquefort if a strong flavor is required and Danish for a milder result.

Camembert
This cheese is made from cow's milk. It has a mild, creamy taste with a slight acidic edge that gets milder with age.

Feta
This soft Greek cheese is rindless, white in color and has a crumbly texture. It is slightly sour, piquant and quite salty to the taste.

Goat cheese
Fresh goat cheese is soft and creamy. As it ages, the cheese becomes harder and the flavor intensifies.

Mozzarella
A unique Italian cheese made from cow's milk, mozzarella has a mild, creamy taste and an unusual spongy texture.

Parmesan
A hard cheese from Italy with a wonderful, distinctive flavor. It is usually grated or shaved wafer-thin. Buy it fresh as the pre-grated cheese sold commercially often lacks the true flavor.

Stilton
An English semi-hard cheese with blue veins, Stilton has a soft, moist texture and a strong flavor.

Tofu
This is an unfermented bean curd made from soy beans. It absorbs flavors readily and is frequently marinated before use. Various forms are available, from soft silken tofu to a firm type which can be cubed and sautéed.

Equipment

Stocking up on every item in your local cookware store will not make you a better cook, but some basic items are definitely worth investing in.

A few good saucepans in various sizes and with tight-fitting lids are a must. Heavy-bottomed and nonstick pans are best. A large nonstick frying pan is invaluable for the quick cook. The food cooks faster when spread over a wider surface area. For the same reason, a good wok is essential. I suggest using a large saucepan or frying pan when the recipe calls for occasional stirring, and a wok for continuous movement, such as stir-frying.

Good-quality knives can halve your preparation time, but more importantly, a really sharp knife is safer than a blunt one. You can do yourself a lot of damage if your hand slips when you are pressing down hard with a blunt knife. For basic, day-to-day use, choose a good chopping knife, a small vegetable knife and a long, serrated bread knife. If possible, store knives safely in well-secured, slotted racks. Drawer storage is not good for knives as the blades can easily become damaged when they are knocked around. If you do have to keep knives in a drawer, make sure they are stored with their handles toward the front for safe lifting and keep the blades protected in some way. Good, sharp knives are essential and indispensable pieces of kitchen equipment, so it is worth taking care of them.

A few of the recipes in this book call for the use of a food processor or blender, which does save time and effort but is not strictly necessary. Some essential pieces of kitchen equipment which almost seem too obvious to mention, include chopping boards, a colander, a strainer, a grater, a whisk and some means of extracting citrus juice, be this a squeezer or a juicer.

For the cook who likes to cook speedily and efficiently, where you store your equipment is an important factor to consider. I use my stove as the pivot around which most of the action takes place. Pots, pans, whisks, spoons and strainers hang conveniently overhead within easy reach, a chopping board is on an adjacent work surface, and ceramic pots hold a variety of wooden spoons, spatulas, ladles, scissors, peelers and other kitchen utensils, again all within easy reach.

wooden spatula

ladle

scissors

knives and peelers

vegetable knife

bread knife

whisks

slotted
spoon

serving
spoon

grater

chopping
board

colander

wok

saucepans

frying pan

Make a Meal of it

The recipes in this book, although conceived as fast food, are equally suitable for entertaining. In fact, the ease and speed of preparation makes them the perfect choice when entertaining, allowing the cook more time to enjoy the company instead of being confined to the kitchen. Most of the recipes make a satisfying meal when served alone or with a simple side salad, while others may require a side order of pasta, rice or potatoes. Should you wish to serve a number of courses, I have compiled a few simple-to-make appetizers and desserts, followed by a selection of menus suggesting the appropriate dishes with which to serve them.

APPETIZERS

Lightly poached asparagus with sour cream and lemon.

Warm focaccia bread accompanied by olive oil, Kosher salt and black olives.

Broiled cherry tomatoes served with salad and basil leaves, drizzled with a little dressing.

Crudités of celery, carrot, baby corn and snow peas served with mayonnaise with a little pesto stirred through.

Thin slices of French bread, topped with tapenade (black olive paste) and mozzarella, then broiled and served hot.

Pre-made hummus and tzatziki served as dips with strips of warm pita bread and black olives.

Chopped fresh tomatoes and onion flavored with chopped fresh cilantro, and served with poppadums.

Desserts

Slices of sticky ginger cake warmed through in the microwave and served with a little maple syrup and cream.

Fresh summer berries, sprinkled with Kirsch and vanilla sugar, served with sour cream or plain yogurt.

Sweetened, whipped cream flavored with passionfruit and served on banana slices. Add amaretti biscuits for contrast.

A slice of Swiss roll topped with a scoop of ice cream, covered in stiff meringue and broiled until golden.

Banana slices and orange segments topped with a little apricot jam, wrapped in foil and baked in a hot oven for 10 minutes. Serve with cream.

Fresh blackberries crushed lightly with a fork and gently folded into softly whipped cream. Add a drizzle of Cassis (optional) and sugar to taste.

Brandy-snap baskets filled with raspberries and peach slices, topped with a swirl of cream and a sprig of mint.

Ripe plums, halved, sprinkled with brandy and filled with mascarpone cheese. The plums are topped with chopped nuts and brown sugar, then broiled until the sugar has melted.

Menus for Entertaining

When you have guests to feed, expand your 15-minute vegetarian main course into an impressive meal. The menu suggestions below feature main course 15-minute vegetarian meals accompanied by quick-and-easy appetizers, accompaniments and desserts.

Menu 1

Warm focaccia bread with Kosher salt and olives

Asparagus Rolls with Herb Butter Sauce

Lentil Stir-fry served with a green salad

Summer berries with Kirsch and vanilla sugar

Menu 2

Broiled cherry tomato and basil salad

Mushrooms with Leeks and Stilton

Potato, Broccoli and Red Bell Pepper Stir-fry

Baked banana and orange segments

Menu 3

Poached asparagus with crème fraîche and lemon

Crusty Rolls with Zucchini and Saffron

Red Fried Rice

Warm ginger cake with maple syrup

Menu 4

French bread slices with tapenade and mozzarella

Lemon and Parmesan Cappellini with Herb Bread

Fresh Spinach and Avocado Salad

Banana and amaretti with passionfruit cream

Menu 5

Fresh tomato and cilantro with poppadoms

Bengali-style Vegetables

Cumin-spiced Large Zucchini and Spinach

Spiced potato and cauliflower Fresh fruit

Menu 6

Crudités with mayonnaise dip

Potato, Spinach and Pine Nut Gratin

Vegetable Kebabs with Mustard and Honey

Broiled mascarpone plums

Deep-fried Zucchini with Chili Sauce

Crunchy coated zucchini are great served with a fiery tomato sauce.

Serves 2

INGREDIENTS
1 tbsp olive oil
1 onion, finely chopped
1 red chili, seeded and finely diced
2 tsp hot chili powder
14 oz can chopped tomatoes
1 vegetable bouillon cube
¼ cup hot water
1 lb zucchini
⅔ cup milk
½ cup all-purpose flour
oil for deep-frying
salt and freshly ground black pepper

TO SERVE
lettuce leaves
watercress sprigs
slices of seeded bread
thyme sprigs, to garnish

zucchini

chopped tomatoes

onion

red chili

all-purpose flour

bouillon cube

milk

chili powder

1 Heat the oil in a pan. Add the onion, and cook for 2–3 minutes. Add the chili. Stir in the chili powder, and cook for 30 seconds.

2 Add the tomatoes. Crumble in the bouillon cube, and stir in the water. Cover and cook for 10 minutes.

3 Meanwhile, remove the ends from the zucchini. Cut them into ¼ in slices.

4 Pour the milk into one shallow dish, and spread out the flour in another. Dip the zucchini first in the milk, then into the flour, until well-coated.

5 Heat the oil for deep-frying to 350°F or until a cube of bread, when added to the oil, browns in 30–45 seconds. Add the zucchini slices in batches, and deep-fry for 3–4 minutes until crisp. Drain on paper towels.

6 Place two or three lettuce leaves on each serving plate. Add a few sprigs of watercress, and fan out the bread slices to one side. Season the sauce, spoon some on to each plate, top with the zucchini and garnish with the sprigs of thyme. Serve at once with a crisp salad and bread.

Cumin-spiced Large Zucchini and Spinach

A great way to enjoy the giant zucchini that escaped in the garden is with spinach and cream.

Serves 2

INGREDIENTS
1 lb zucchini
2 tbsp vegetable oil
2 tsp cumin seeds
1 small red chili, seeded and
  finely chopped
2 tbsp water
2 oz tender, young spinach leaves
6 tbsp light cream
salt and freshly ground black pepper

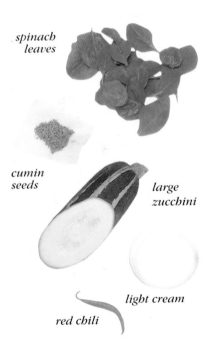

spinach
leaves

cumin
seeds

large
zucchini

light cream

red chili

1 Peel the zucchini, and cut it in half. Scoop out the seeds. Cut the flesh into ¹/₂ in cubes.

2 Heat the oil in a large frying pan. Add the cumin seeds and the chopped chili. Cook for 1 minute.

3 Add the zucchini and water to the pan. Cover with foil or a lid, and simmer for 8 minutes, stirring occasionally, until the zucchini is just tender. Remove the cover, and cook for 2 minutes more or until most of the water has evaporated.

4 Put the spinach leaves in a colander. Rinse well under cold water, drain and pat dry with paper towels. Tear into rough pieces.

5 Add the spinach to the zucchini. Replace the cover, and cook gently for 1 minute.

6 Stir in the cream, and cook over a high heat for 2 minutes. Add salt and pepper to taste, and serve. An Indian rice dish would be a good accompaniment. As an alternative, serve with naan bread.

Chili Beans with Basmati Rice

Red kidney beans, tomatoes and chili make a great combination. Serve with pasta or pita bread instead of rice, if you prefer.

Serves 4

INGREDIENTS
2 cups basmati rice
2 tbsp olive oil
1 large onion, chopped
1 garlic clove, crushed
1 tbsp hot chili powder
1 tbsp all-purpose flour
1 tbsp tomato paste
14 oz can chopped tomatoes
14 oz can red kidney beans, drained
²/₃ cup hot vegetable stock
chopped fresh parsley, to garnish
salt and freshly ground black pepper

basmati rice

chopped tomatoes

chili powder

onion   tomato paste

garlic clove

stock cube   red kidney beans   all-purpose flour

1 Wash the rice several times under cold running water. Drain well. Bring a large pan of water to a boil. Add the rice, and cook for 10–12 minutes, until tender. Meanwhile, heat the oil in a frying pan. Add the onion and garlic, and cook for 2 minutes.

2 Stir the chili powder and flour into the onion and garlic mixture. Cook for 2 minutes, stirring frequently.

3 Stir in the tomato paste and chopped tomatoes. Rinse the kidney beans under cold water, drain well, and add to the pan with the hot vegetable stock. Cover and cook for 12 minutes, stirring occasionally.

4 Season the chili sauce with salt and pepper. Drain the rice, and serve at once, with the chili beans, sprinkled with a little chopped fresh parsley.

Spicy Cauliflower and Potato Salad

A delicious, cold vegetable salad with a hot and spicy dressing.

Serves 2–3

INGREDIENTS
1 cauliflower
2 potatoes
1½ tsp caraway seeds
1 tsp ground coriander
½ tsp hot chili powder
juice of 1 lemon
4 tbsp olive oil
salt and freshly ground black pepper

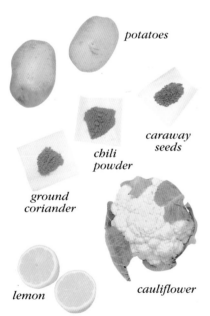

potatoes

caraway
seeds

chili
powder

ground
coriander

lemon

cauliflower

1 Break the cauliflower into small florets. Peel the potatoes, and cut them into chunks.

2 Bring a large pan of water to a boil. Add the cauliflower florets and potato chunks, and cook for 8 minutes until they are just tender.

3 Meanwhile, heat a nonstick frying pan. Add the caraway seeds, and fry, shaking the pan constantly, for 1 minute. Turn the roasted seeds into a bowl, and add the ground coriander and chili powder, with salt and pepper to taste. Stir in the lemon juice and olive oil. Mix to a paste.

4 Drain the vegetables well. Add them to the bowl, and toss to coat in the chili dressing. Serve at once, with hot pita bread or brown rice.

Bengali-style Vegetables

A hot, dry curry using spices that do not require long, slow cooking.

Serves 4

INGREDIENTS
½ cauliflower, broken into
 small florets
1 large potato, peeled and cut into
 1 in dice
4 oz green beans, trimmed
2 zucchini, halved lengthwise
 and sliced
2 green chilies
1 in piece of fresh ginger, peeled
½ cup plain yogurt
2 tsp ground coriander
½ tsp ground turmeric
2 tbsp ghee or vegetable oil
½ tsp garam masala
1 tsp cumin seeds
2 tsp sugar
pinch each of ground cloves,
 ground cinnamon and
 ground cardamom
salt and freshly ground black pepper

1 Bring a large pan of water to a boil. Add the cauliflower and potato, and cook for 5 minutes. Add the beans and zucchini, and cook for 2–3 minutes.

2 Meanwhile, cut the chilies in half, remove the seeds, and coarsely chop the flesh. Finely chop the ginger. Mix the chilies and ginger in a small bowl.

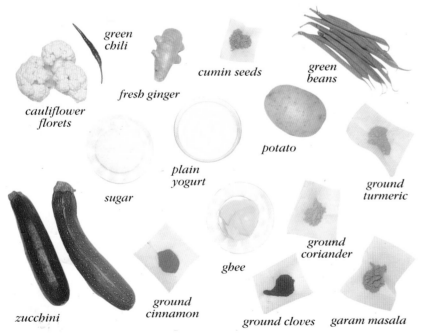

green
chili

cumin seeds

green
beans

fresh ginger

cauliflower
florets

plain
yogurt

potato

sugar

ground
turmeric

zucchini

ground
cinnamon

ghee

ground
cloves

ground
coriander

garam masala

3 Drain the vegetables, and turn them into a bowl. Add the chili and ginger mixture, with the yogurt, ground coriander and turmeric. Season with plenty of salt and pepper, and mix well.

4 Heat the ghee or oil in a large frying pan. Add the vegetable mixture, and cook over a high heat for 2 minutes, stirring from time to time.

5 Stir in the garam masala and cumin seeds, and cook for 2 minutes.

6 Stir in the sugar and remaining spices, and cook for 1 minute or until all the liquid has evaporated.

COOK'S TIP
If ghee is not available, you can clarify your own butter. Melt ¹/₄ cup butter slowly in a small pan. Remove from the heat, and leave for about 5 minutes. Then pour off the clear yellow clarified butter, leaving the sediment in the pan.

Vegetable Fajita

A colorful medley of mushrooms and bell peppers in a spicy sauce, wrapped in tortillas and served with creamy guacamole.

Serves 2

INGREDIENTS
1 onion
1 red bell pepper
1 green bell pepper
1 yellow bell pepper
1 garlic clove, crushed
8 oz mushrooms
6 tbsp vegetable oil
2 tbsp medium chili powder
salt and freshly ground black pepper

FOR THE GUACAMOLE
1 ripe avocado
1 shallot, coarsely chopped
1 green chili, seeded and
 coarsely chopped
juice of 1 lime

TO SERVE
4–6 flour tortillas, warmed
1 lime, cut into wedges
cilantro sprigs

green bell pepper

yellow bell pepper

red bell pepper

mushrooms

green chili

garlic clove

shallot

avocado

lime

chili powder

onion

1 Slice the onion. Cut the bell peppers in half, remove the seeds, and cut the flesh into strips. Combine the onion and peppers in a bowl. Add the crushed garlic, and mix lightly.

2 Remove the mushroom stalks. Save for making stock, or discard. Slice the mushroom caps, and add to the pepper mixture in the bowl. Mix the oil and chili powder in a cup, pour over the vegetable mixture, and stir well. Set aside.

3 Make the guacamole. Cut the avocado in half, and remove the pit and the peel. Put the flesh into a food processor or blender with the shallot, green chili and lime juice. Process for 1 minute until smooth. Scrape into a small bowl, cover tightly, and put in the fridge to chill until required.

4 Heat a frying pan or wok until very hot. Add the marinated vegetables, and stir-fry over a high heat for 5–6 minutes until the mushrooms and pepper are just tender. Season well. Spoon a little of the filling on to each tortilla, and roll up. Garnish with fresh cilantro, and serve with the guacamole and lime wedges.

Curried Eggs

Hard-boiled eggs are served on a bed of mild, creamy sauce with a hint of curry.

Serves 2

INGREDIENTS

4 eggs
1 tbsp sunflower oil
1 small onion, finely chopped
1 in piece of fresh ginger,
  peeled and grated
$\frac{1}{2}$ tsp ground cumin
$\frac{1}{2}$ tsp garam masala
$1\frac{1}{2}$ tbsp tomato paste
2 tsp tandoori paste
2 tsp lemon juice
$\frac{1}{4}$ cup light cream
1 tbsp chopped fresh cilantro
salt and freshly ground black pepper
cilantro sprigs, to garnish

eggs   fresh ginger   garam masala   fresh cilantro

ground cumin   light cream

tomato paste   tandoori paste   lemon   onion

1 Put the eggs in a pan of water. Bring to a boil, lower the heat, and simmer for 10 minutes.

2 Meanwhile, heat the oil in a frying pan. Cook the onion for 2–3 minutes. Add the ginger, and cook for 1 minute.

3 Stir in the ground cumin, garam masala, tomato paste, tandoori paste, lemon juice and cream. Cook for 1–2 minutes, then stir in the cilantro. Add salt and pepper to taste.

4 Drain the eggs, remove the shells, and cut each egg in half. Spoon the sauce into a serving bowl, top with the eggs, and garnish with the cilantro sprigs. Serve at once.

Breaded Eggplant with Hot Vinaigrette

Crisp on the outside, beautifully tender within, these eggplant slices taste wonderful with a spicy dressing flavored with chili and capers.

COOK'S TIP
When serving a salad with a warm dressing, use robust leaves that will stand up to the heat.

Serves 2

INGREDIENTS
1 large eggplant
1/2 cup all-purpose flour
2 eggs, beaten
2 cups fresh white bread crumbs
vegetable oil for frying
1 head radicchio
salt and freshly ground black pepper

FOR THE DRESSING
2 tbsp olive oil
1 garlic clove, crushed
1 tbsp capers, drained
1 tbsp white wine vinegar
1 tbsp chili oil

eggplant

bread crumbs

all-purpose flour

eggs

radicchio

capers

white wine vinegar

garlic clove

1 Remove the ends from the eggplant. Cut it into 1/4 in slices. Set aside.

2 Season the flour with a generous amount of salt and black pepper. Spread out in a shallow dish. Pour the beaten eggs into a second dish. Spread out the bread crumbs in a third.

3 Dip the eggplant slices in the flour, then in the beaten egg and finally in the bread crumbs, patting them on to make an even coating.

4 Pour vegetable oil into a large frying pan to a depth of about 1/4 in. Heat the oil, then fry the eggplant slices for 3–4 minutes, turning once. Drain well on paper towels.

5 Heat the olive oil in a small pan. Add the garlic and the capers, and cook over gentle heat for 1 minute. Increase the heat, add the vinegar, and cook for 30 seconds. Stir in the chili oil, and remove the pan from the heat.

6 Arrange the radicchio leaves on two plates. Top with the hot eggplant slices. Drizzle over the vinaigrette, and serve.

Double Tomato Tagliatelle

Sun-dried tomatoes add pungency to this dish, while the broiled fresh tomatoes add bite.

Serves 4

INGREDIENTS
3 tbsp olive oil
1 garlic clove, crushed
1 small onion, chopped
¼ cup dry white wine
6 sun-dried tomatoes, chopped
2 tbsp chopped fresh parsley
½ cup pitted black olives, halved
1 lb fresh tagliatelle
4 tomatoes, halved
Parmesan cheese, to serve
salt and freshly ground black pepper

tomatoes

parsley

garlic clove

sun-dried tomatoes

tagliatelle

dry white wine

onion

black olives

Parmesan cheese

COOK'S TIP

It is essential to buy Parmesan in a piece for this dish. Find a good source – fresh Parmesan should not be unacceptably hard – and shave or grate it yourself. The flavor will be much more intense than that of the pre-grated product.

1 Heat 2 tbsp of the oil in a pan. Add the garlic and onion, and cook for 2–3 minutes, stirring occasionally. Add the wine, sun-dried tomatoes and the parsley. Cook for 2 minutes. Stir in the black olives.

2 Bring a large pan of salted water to a boil. Add the fresh tagliatelle, and cook for 2–3 minutes until just tender. Preheat the broiler.

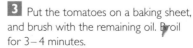

3 Put the tomatoes on a baking sheet, and brush with the remaining oil. Broil for 3–4 minutes.

4 Drain the pasta, return it to the pan, and toss with the sauce. Serve with the broiled tomatoes, freshly ground black pepper and shavings of Parmesan.

Penne with Fennel, Tomato and Blue Cheese

The anise flavor of the fennel makes it the perfect partner for tomato, especially when topped with blue cheese.

Serves 2

INGREDIENTS
1 fennel bulb
8 oz penne or other dried
  pasta shapes
2 tbsp extra virgin olive oil
1 shallot, finely chopped
1¼ cups strained tomatoes
pinch of sugar
1 tsp chopped fresh oregano
4 oz blue cheese
salt and freshly ground black pepper

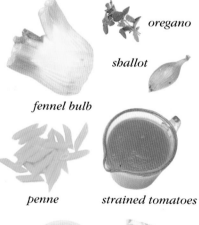

oregano

shallot

fennel bulb

penne *strained tomatoes*

sugar *blue cheese*

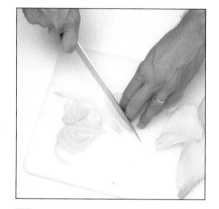

1 Cut the fennel bulb in half. Cut away the hard core and root. Slice the fennel thinly, then cut the slices into strips.

2 Bring a large pan of salted water to a boil. Add the pasta, and cook for 10–12 minutes until just tender.

3 Meanwhile, heat the oil in a small saucepan. Add the fennel and shallot, and cook for 2–3 minutes over a high heat, stirring occasionally.

4 Add the tomatoes, sugar and oregano. Cover the pan, and simmer gently for 10–12 minutes, until the fennel is tender. Add salt and pepper to taste. Drain the pasta, and return it to the pan. Toss with the sauce. Serve with blue cheese crumbled over the top.

Lemon and Parmesan Capellini with Herb Bread

Cream is thickened with Parmesan and flavored with lemon to make a superb sauce for pasta.

Serves 2

INGREDIENTS

½ whole wheat stick
¼ cup butter, softened
1 garlic clove, crushed
2 tbsp chopped fresh herbs
8 oz dried or fresh capellini
1 cup light cream
3 oz Parmesan cheese, grated
finely grated rind of 1 lemon
salt and freshly ground black pepper

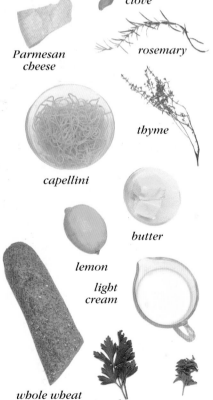

garlic clove

Parmesan cheese

rosemary

thyme

capellini

butter

lemon

light cream

whole wheat stick   *parsley*   *oregano*

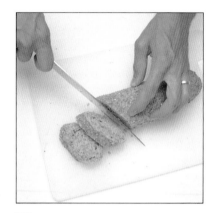

1 Preheat the oven to 400°F. Cut the whole wheat stick into thick slices.

2 Put the butter in a bowl, and beat with the garlic and herbs. Spread thickly over each slice of bread.

3 Reassemble the stick. Wrap in foil. Support on a baking sheet, and bake for 10 minutes.

4 Meanwhile, bring a large pan of water to a boil, and cook the pasta until just tender. Dried pasta will take 10–12 minutes; fresh pasta will be ready in 2–3 minutes.

5 Pour the cream into another pan, and bring to a boil. Stir in the Parmesan and lemon rind. The sauce should thicken in about 30 seconds.

6 Drain the pasta, return it to the pan, and toss with the sauce. Season to taste, and sprinkle with a little chopped fresh parsley and grated lemon rind, if desired. Serve with the hot herb bread.

Summer Pasta Salad

Tender, young vegetables in a light dressing make a delicious lunch.

Serves 2–3

INGREDIENTS
8 oz fusilli or other dried
  pasta shapes
4 oz baby carrots, trimmed
  and halved
4 oz baby corn, halved lengthwise
2 oz snow peas
4 oz young asparagus spears,
  trimmed
4 scallions, trimmed and shredded
2 tsp white wine vinegar
4 tbsp extra virgin olive oil
1 tbsp whole-grain mustard
salt and freshly ground black pepper

scallions

*young
asparagus*

fusilli

*baby
carrots*

*whole-grain
mustard*

baby corn

*white wine
vinegar*

snow peas

1 Bring a large pan of salted water to a boil. Add the pasta, and cook for about 10–12 minutes, until just tender. Meanwhile, cook the carrots and corn in a second pan of boiling salted water for 5 minutes.

2 Add the snow peas and asparagus spears to the carrots and corn, and cook for 2–3 minutes more. Drain all of the vegetables, and refresh under cold running water. Drain again.

3 Turn the vegetable mixture into a mixing bowl, add the scallions, and toss well together.

4 Drain the pasta, refresh it under cold running water, and drain again. Toss with the vegetables. Mix the vinegar, olive oil and mustard in a jar. Add salt and pepper to taste. Close the jar tightly, and shake well. Pour the dressing over the salad. Toss well, and serve.

Five-spice Vegetable Noodles

Vary this vegetable stir-fry by substituting mushrooms, bamboo shoots, beansprouts, snow peas or water chestnuts for some or all of the vegetables suggested below.

Serves 2–3

INGREDIENTS
8 oz dried egg noodles
2 tbsp sesame oil
2 carrots
1 celery stalk
1 small fennel bulb
2 zucchini, halved and sliced
1 red chili, seeded and chopped
1 in piece of fresh ginger, grated
1 garlic clove, crushed
1½ tsp Chinese five-spice powder
½ tsp ground cinnamon
4 scallions, sliced
¼ cup warm water
1 red chili, seed ed and sliced,
 to garnish (optional)

celery stalk

carrots

garlic clove

fennel bulb

egg noodles

zucchini

five-spice powder

scallions

cinnamon

fresh ginger

1 Bring a large pan of salted water to a boil. Add the noodles, and cook for 2–3 minutes until just tender. Drain the noodles, return them to the pan, and toss in a little of the oil. Set aside.

2 Cut the carrot and celery into julienne. Cut the fennel bulb in half, and cut out the hard core. Cut into slices. Then cut the slices into julienne.

3 Heat the remaining oil in a wok or frying pan until very hot. Add all the vegetables, including the chili, and stir-fry for 7–8 minutes.

4 Add the ginger and garlic, and stir-fry for 2 minutes. Then add the spices. Cook for 1 minute. Add the scallions. Stir-fry for 1 minute. Pour in the warm water, and cook for 1 minute. Stir in the noodles, and toss well together. Serve sprinkled with sliced red chili, if desired.

Mushroom Bolognese

A quick – and exceedingly tasty – vegetarian version of the classic Italian meat dish.

Serves 4

INGREDIENTS
1 lb mushrooms
1 tbsp olive oil
1 onion, chopped
1 garlic clove, crushed
1 tbsp tomato paste
14 oz can chopped tomatoes
3 tbsp chopped fresh oregano
1 lb fresh pasta
Parmesan cheese, to serve
salt and freshly ground black pepper

mushrooms

chopped tomatoes

oregano

garlic clove

pasta

onion

Parmesan cheese

tomato paste

1 Trim the mushroom stems neatly. Then cut each mushroom into quarters.

2 Heat the oil in a large pan. Add the chopped onion and garlic, and cook for 2–3 minutes.

3 Add the mushrooms to the pan, and cook over a high heat for 3–4 minutes, stirring occasionally.

4 Stir in the tomato paste, chopped tomatoes and 1 tbsp of the oregano. Lower the heat, cover, and cook for about 5 minutes.

5 Meanwhile, bring a large pan of salted water to a boil. Cook the pasta for 2–3 minutes until just tender.

COOK'S TIP
If you prefer to use dried pasta, make this the first thing that you cook. It will take 10–12 minutes, during which time you can make the mushroom mixture. Use 12 oz dried pasta.

6 Season the bolognese sauce with salt and pepper. Drain the pasta, turn it into a bowl, and add the mushroom mixture. Toss to mix well. Serve in individual bowls, topped with shavings of fresh Parmesan and the remaining chopped fresh oregano.

Fried Noodles with Beansprouts and Asparagus

Soft fried noodles contrast beautifully with crisp beansprouts and asparagus.

Serves 2

INGREDIENTS
4 oz dried egg noodles
4 tbsp vegetable oil
1 small onion, chopped
1 in piece of fresh ginger,
   peeled and grated
2 garlic cloves, crushed
6 oz young asparagus spears,
   trimmed
4 oz beansprouts
4 scallions, sliced
3 tbsp soy sauce
salt and freshly ground black pepper

onion

scallions

garlic cloves

fresh ginger

soy sauce

egg noodles

beansprouts

asparagus spears

1 Bring a pan of salted water to a boil. Add the noodles, and cook for 2–3 minutes, until just tender. Drain, and toss in 2 tbsp of the oil.

2 Heat the remaining oil in a wok or frying pan until very hot. Add the onion, ginger and garlic, and stir-fry for 2–3 minutes. Add the asparagus, and stir-fry for 2–3 minutes more.

3 Add the noodles and beansprouts, and stir-fry for 2 minutes.

4 Stir in the scallions and soy sauce. Season to taste, adding salt sparingly as the soy sauce will probably supply enough salt in itself. Stir-fry for 1 minute, then serve at once.

Pasta with Cilantro and Broiled Eggplant

Pasta with a piquant sauce of cilantro and lime – a variation on the classic pesto – is superb served with broiled eggplant.

Serves 2

INGREDIENTS
½ oz cilantro leaves
2 tbsp pine nuts
2 tbsp freshly grated Parmesan cheese
3 garlic cloves
juice of ½ lime
7 tbsp olive oil
8 oz dried cellentani or other pasta shapes
1 large eggplant
salt and freshly ground black pepper

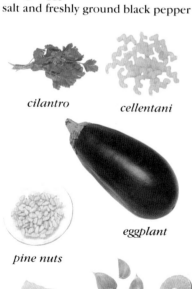

cilantro   cellentani

eggplant

pine nuts

Parmesan cheese   garlic cloves   lime

1 Process the cilantro leaves, pine nuts, Parmesan, garlic, lime juice and 4 tbsp of the olive oil in a food processor or blender for 30 seconds until almost smooth. Bring a large pan of salted water to a boil. Add the pasta, and cook for 10–12 minutes until cooked but still firm to the bite.

2 Meanwhile, cut the eggplant in half lengthwise. Then cut each half into ¼ in slices. Spread out on a baking sheet, brush with the remaining oil, and season well with salt and black pepper.

3 Broil the eggplant slices for about 4 minutes. Turn them over, and brush with the remaining oil. Season as before. Broil for 4 minutes more.

4 Drain the pasta, turn it into a bowl, and toss with the cilantro sauce. Serve with the broiled eggplant slices.

Parmesan and Poached Egg Salad with Croûtons

Soft poached eggs, hot garlic croûtons and cool, crisp salad leaves make an unforgettable combination.

Serves 2

INGREDIENTS
1/2 small loaf white bread
5 tbsp extra virgin olive oil
2 eggs
4 oz mixed salad leaves
2 garlic cloves, crushed
1/2 tbsp white wine vinegar
1 oz Parmesan cheese

Parmesan cheese

mixed salad leaves

white bread

garlic cloves

eggs

1 Remove the crust from the bread. Cut the bread into 1 in cubes.

2 Heat 2 tbsp of the oil in a frying pan. Cook the bread for about 5 minutes, tossing the cubes occasionally, until they are golden brown.

3 Meanwhile, bring a pan of water to a boil. Carefully slide in the eggs, one at a time. Gently poach the eggs for 4 minutes until lightly cooked.

4 Divide the salad leaves between two plates. Remove the croûtons from the pan, and arrange them over the leaves. Wipe the pan clean with paper towels.

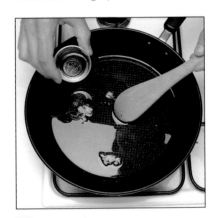

5 Heat the remaining oil in the pan, add the garlic and vinegar, and cook over high heat for 1 minute. Pour the warm dressing over each salad.

COOK'S TIP
Add a dash of vinegar to the water before poaching the eggs. This helps to keep the whites together. To make sure that a poached egg has a good shape, swirl the water with a spoon, whirlpool-fashion, before sliding in the egg.

6 Place a poached egg on each salad. Sprinkle with shavings of Parmesan and freshly ground black pepper, if desired.

Classic Greek Salad

If you have ever visited Greece, you'll know that a Greek salad with a chunk of bread makes a delicious, filling meal.

Serves 4

INGREDIENTS
1 Romaine lettuce
$^1/_2$ cucumber, halved lengthwise
4 tomatoes
8 scallions
$^1/_3$ cup Greek black olives
4 oz feta cheese
6 tbsp white wine vinegar
$^1/_2$ cup extra virgin olive oil
salt and freshly ground black pepper

tomatoes

Romaine lettuce

feta cheese

white wine vinegar

black olives

cucumber

scallions

1 Tear the lettuce leaves into pieces, and place them in a large mixing bowl. Slice the cucumber, and add to the bowl.

2 Cut the tomatoes into wedges, and put them into the bowl.

3 Slice the scallions. Add them to the bowl with the olives, and toss well.

4 Cut the feta cheese into cubes, and add to the salad.

5 Put the vinegar, olive oil and seasoning into a small bowl, and whisk well. Pour the dressing over the salad, and toss to combine. Serve at once, with olives and chunks of bread, if desired.

COOK'S TIP
The salad can be assembled in advance and chilled, but add the lettuce and dressing just before serving. Keep the dressing at room temperature as chilling deadens its flavor.

Belgian Endive, Fruit and Nut Salad

Mildly bitter endive is wonderful with sweet fruit, and is especially delicious when complemented by a creamy curry sauce.

Serves 4

INGREDIENTS
3 tbsp mayonnaise
1 tbsp strained, plain yogurt
1 tbsp mild curry paste
6 tbsp light cream
$1/2$ iceberg lettuce
2 heads of Belgian endive
$1/2$ cup cashews
$1^{1}/_{4}$ cups flaked coconut
2 red apples
$1/2$ cup currants

currants

iceberg lettuce

cashews

curry paste   mayonnaise

red apples

light cream   flaked coconut

Belgian endive

1 Mix the mayonnaise, yogurt, curry paste and light cream in a small bowl. Cover, and chill until required.

2 Tear the iceberg lettuce into pieces, and put into a salad bowl.

3 Cut the root end off each head of Belgian endive, and discard. Slice the endive, and add it to the salad bowl.

4 Preheat the broiler. Toast the cashews for 2 minutes until they are golden. Turn into a bowl, and set aside. Spread out the coconut flakes on a baking sheet. Broil for 1 minute.

5 Quarter the apples, and cut out the cores. Slice the apples, and add to the lettuce with the cashews, flaked coconut, and currants.

COOK'S TIP
Watch the coconut and cashews very carefully when broiling, as they brown very fast.

6 Spoon the dressing over the salad. Toss lightly, and serve.

Broiled Bell Pepper Salad

Broiled bell peppers are delicious served hot with a sharp dressing. You can also eat them cold.

Serves 2

INGREDIENTS
1 red bell pepper
1 green bell pepper
1 yellow or orange bell pepper
1/2 radicchio, separated into leaves
1/2 frisée, separated into leaves
1 1/2 tsp white wine vinegar
2 tbsp extra virgin olive oil
6 oz goat cheese
salt and freshly ground black pepper

frisée

green bell pepper

red bell pepper

goat cheese

yellow bell pepper

white wine vinegar

radicchio

1 Preheat the broiler. Cut all the bell peppers in half. Cut each half into pieces.

2 Put the pepper pieces on a rack set over a broiler pan. Broil for 10 minutes.

3 Meanwhile, divide the radicchio and frisée leaves between two plates. Chill until required.

4 Mix the vinegar and olive oil in a jar. Add salt and pepper to taste. Close the jar tightly, and shake well.

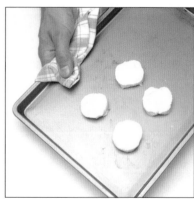

5 Slice the goat cheese, and place on a baking sheet. Broil for 1 minute.

6 Arrange the peppers and broiled goat cheese on the salads. Pour over the dressing, and grind a little extra black pepper over each.

COOK'S TIP
Broil the bell peppers until they just start to blacken around the edges – don't let them burn.

Zucchini, Carrots and Pecans in Pita Bread

Chunks of fried zucchini served with a tangy salad in pita pockets.

Serves 2

INGREDIENTS
2 carrots
¼ cup pecan nuts
4 scallions, sliced
¼ cup strained, plain yogurt
7 tsp olive oil
1 tsp lemon juice
1 tbsp chopped fresh mint
2 zucchini
¼ cup all-purpose flour
2 pita breads
salt and freshly ground black pepper
shredded lettuce, to serve

zucchini

scallions

pecan nuts   lemon

mint

strained,
plain yogurt

carrots

1 Remove the ends from the carrots. Grate them coarsely into a bowl.

2 Stir in the pecans and scallions, and toss well together.

3 In a clean bowl, whisk the yogurt with 1½ tsp of the olive oil, the lemon juice and the fresh mint. Stir the dressing into the carrot mixture, and mix well. Cover, and chill until required.

4 Remove the ends from the zucchini. Cut them diagonally into slices. Season the flour with salt and pepper. Spread it on a plate, and coat the zucchini slices.

COOK'S TIP
Do not fill the pita breads too soon or the carrot mixture will make the bread soggy.

5 Heat the remaining oil in a large frying pan. Add the coated zucchini slices, and cook for 3–4 minutes, turning once, until browned. Drain the zucchini on paper towels.

6 Make a slit in each pita bread to form a pocket. Fill the pitas with the carrot mixture and the zucchini slices. Serve on a bed of shredded lettuce.

Zucchini Puffs with Salad and Balsamic Dressing

This unusual salad consists of deep-fried zucchini, flavored with mint, and served warm on a bed of salad leaves with a balsamic dressing.

Serves 2

INGREDIENTS
1 lb zucchini
1½ cups fresh white bread crumbs
1 egg
pinch of cayenne pepper
1 tbsp chopped fresh mint
oil for deep-frying
3 tbsp balsamic vinegar
3 tbsp extra virgin olive oil
7 oz mixed salad leaves
salt and freshly ground black pepper

zucchini

white bread crumbs

balsamic vinegar

mixed salad leaves

egg *mint*

1 Remove the ends from the zucchini. Coarsely grate them, and put into a colander. Squeeze out the excess water. Then put the zucchini into a bowl.

2 Add the bread crumbs, egg, cayenne, mint and seasoning. Mix well.

3 Shape the zucchini mixture into balls, about the size of walnuts.

4 Heat the oil for deep-frying to 350°F or until a cube of bread, when added to the oil, browns in 30–40 seconds. Deep-fry the zucchini balls in batches for 2–3 minutes. Drain on paper towels.

5 Whisk the vinegar and oil together, and season well.

6 Put the salad leaves in a bowl, and pour over the dressing. Add the zucchini puffs, and toss lightly together. Serve at once, while the puffs are still crisp.

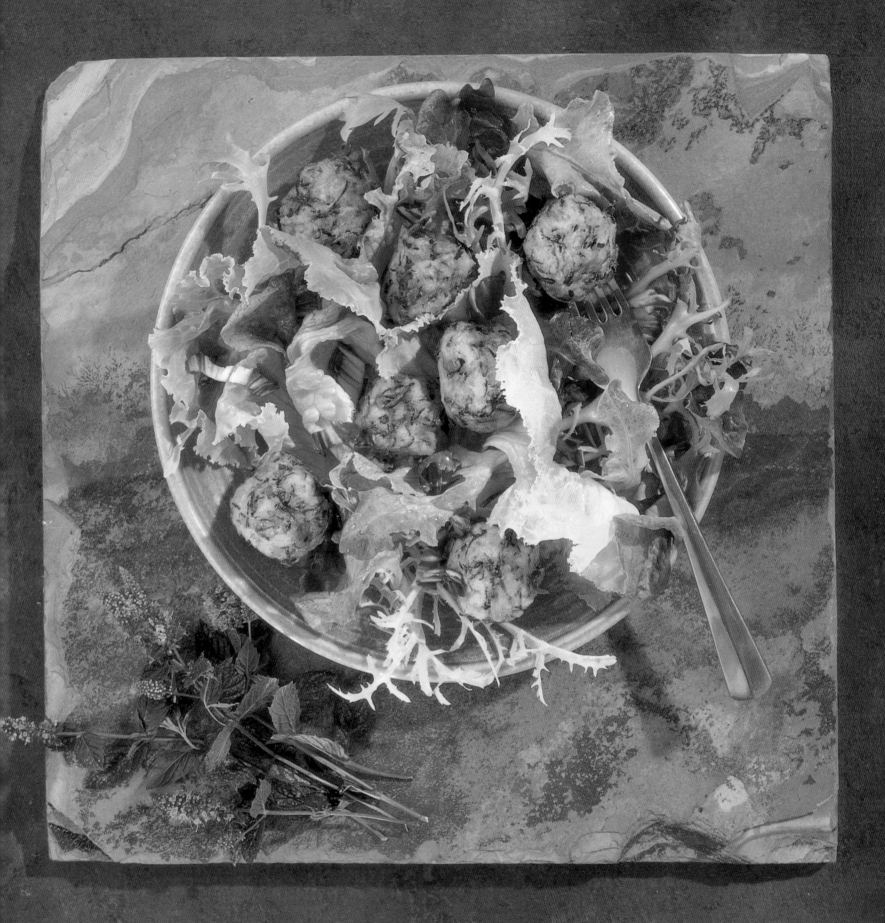

Vegetable and Satay Salad

Baby new potatoes, tender vegetables and crunchy chick-peas are smothered in a creamy peanut dressing.

Serves 4

INGREDIENTS

1 lb baby new potatoes
1 small head cauliflower, broken into small florets
8 oz green beans, trimmed
14 oz can chick-peas, drained
4 oz watercress sprigs
4 oz beansprouts
8 scallions, sliced
4 tbsp crunchy peanut butter
$^2/_3$ cup hot water
1 tsp chili sauce
2 tsp brown sugar
1 tsp soy sauce
1 tsp lime juice

cauliflower

watercress

soy sauce

scallions

crunchy peanut butter

brown sugar

chick-peas

beansprouts

chili sauce

lime

green beans

baby new potatoes

1 Put the potatoes into a pan, and add water just to cover. Bring to a boil, and cook for 10–12 minutes or until the potatoes are just tender when pierced with the point of a sharp knife. Drain, and refresh under cold running water. Drain once again.

2 Meanwhile, bring another pan of salted water to a boil. Add the cauliflower, and cook for 5 minutes. Then add the beans, and cook for 5 minutes more. Drain both vegetables, refresh under cold water, and drain once more.

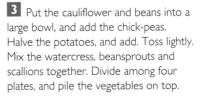

3 Put the cauliflower and beans into a large bowl, and add the chick-peas. Halve the potatoes, and add. Toss lightly. Mix the watercress, beansprouts and scallions together. Divide among four plates, and pile the vegetables on top.

4 Put the peanut butter into a bowl, and stir in the water. Add the chili sauce, brown sugar, soy sauce and lime juice. Whisk well, then drizzle the dressing over the vegetables.

Fresh Spinach and Avocado Salad

Young, tender spinach leaves make a change from lettuce and are delicious served with avocado, cherry tomatoes and radishes in a tofu sauce.

Serves 2–3

INGREDIENTS
1 large avocado
juice of 1 lime
8 oz fresh baby spinach leaves
4 oz cherry tomatoes
4 scallions, sliced
½ cucumber
2 oz radishes, sliced

FOR THE DRESSING
4 oz soft silken tofu
3 tbsp milk
2 tsp prepared mustard
½ tsp white wine vinegar
pinch of cayenne
salt and freshly ground black pepper

tofu *scallions*

spinach leaves

cherry tomatoes

avocado

white wine vinegar

mustard

cayenne

lime

cucumber

radishes

milk

1 Cut the avocado in half, remove the pit, and strip off the skin. Cut the flesh into slices. Transfer to a plate, drizzle over the lime juice, and set aside.

2 Wash and dry the spinach leaves. Put them in a mixing bowl.

COOK'S TIP
Use soft silken tofu rather than the block variety. It can be found in most supermarkets in the vegetable or refrigerated sections.

3 Cut the larger cherry tomatoes in half, and add all the tomatoes to the mixing bowl, with the scallions. Cut the cucumber into chunks, and add to the bowl with the sliced radishes.

4 Make the dressing. Put the tofu, milk, mustard, wine vinegar and cayenne in a food processor or blender. Add salt and pepper to taste. Process for 30 seconds until smooth. Scrape the dressing into a bowl, and add a little extra milk if you like a thinner dressing. Sprinkle with a little extra cayenne, and garnish with radish roses and herb sprigs, if desired.

Asparagus Rolls with Herb Butter Sauce

For a taste sensation, try tender asparagus spears wrapped in crisp filo pastry. The buttery herb sauce makes the perfect accompaniment.

Serves 2

INGREDIENTS
4 sheets of filo pastry
1/4 cup butter, melted
16 young asparagus spears, trimmed

FOR THE SAUCE
2 shallots, finely chopped
1 bay leaf
2/3 cup dry white wine
6 oz butter, softened
1 tbsp chopped fresh herbs
salt and freshly ground black pepper
chopped chives, to garnish

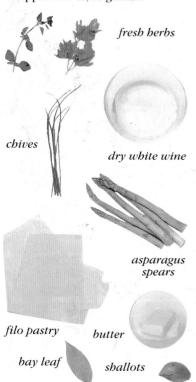

fresh herbs

chives

dry white wine

asparagus spears

filo pastry   *butter*

bay leaf   *shallots*

1 Preheat the oven to 400°F. Cut the filo sheets in half. Brush a half sheet with melted butter. Fold one corner of the sheet down to the bottom edge to give a wedge shape.

2 Lay 4 asparagus spears on top at the longest edge, and roll up toward the shortest edge. Using the remaining filo and asparagus spears, make three more rolls in the same way.

3 Lay the rolls on a greased baking sheet. Brush with the remaining melted butter. Bake in the oven for 8 minutes until golden.

4 Meanwhile, put the shallots, bay leaf and wine into a pan. Cover, and cook over a high heat until the wine is reduced to 3–4 tbsp.

5 Strain the wine mixture into a bowl. Whisk in the butter, a little at a time, until the sauce is smooth and glossy.

6 Stir in the herbs, and add salt and pepper to taste. Return to the pan, and keep the sauce warm. Serve the rolls on individual plates with a salad garnish, if desired. Serve the sauce separately, sprinkled with a few chopped chives.

Tomato Omelet Envelopes

Delicious chive omelet, folded and filled with a tasty tomato mixture and lots of melting Camembert cheese.

Serves 2

INGREDIENTS
1 small onion
4 tomatoes
2 tbsp vegetable oil
4 eggs
2 tbsp chopped fresh chives
4 oz Camembert cheese, rind
  removed and diced
salt and freshly ground black pepper

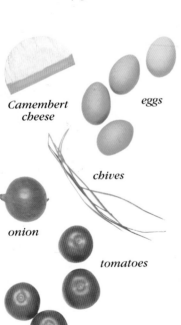

Camembert cheese

eggs

chives

onion

tomatoes

1 Cut the onion in half. Cut each half into thin wedges. Cut the tomatoes into wedges of similar size.

2 Heat 1 tbsp of the oil in a frying pan. Cook the onion for 2 minutes over a moderate heat. Then raise the heat, and add the tomato wedges. Cook for 2 minutes more. Then remove the pan from the heat.

3 Beat the eggs with the chives in a bowl. Add salt and pepper to taste. Heat the remaining oil in an omelet pan. Add half the egg mixture, and tilt the pan to spread thinly. Cook for 1 minute.

4 Flip the omelet over, and cook for 1 minute more. Remove from the pan, and keep hot. Make a second omelet with the remaining egg mixture.

5 Return the tomato mixture to a high heat. Add the cheese, and toss the mixture over the heat for 1 minute.

6 Divide the mixture between the omelets, and fold them over. Serve at once. Add crisp lettuce leaves and chunks of whole wheat bread, if desired.

COOK'S TIP
You may need to wipe the pan clean between the omelets, and reheat a little more oil.

Mushrooms with Leeks and Stilton

Upturned mushrooms make perfect containers for this leek and Stilton filling.

Serves 2–3

INGREDIENTS
1 leek, thinly sliced
6 flat mushrooms
2 garlic cloves, crushed
2 tbsp chopped fresh parsley
1/2 cup butter, softened
4 oz Stilton cheese
freshly ground black pepper
frisée and tomato halves, to garnish

leek

butter

flat mushrooms

parsley

Stilton cheese

garlic cloves

1 Put the leek slices in a small pan with a little water. Cover, and cook for about 5 minutes until tender. Drain. Refresh under cold water, and drain again.

2 Remove the stalks from the flat mushrooms, and set them aside. Put the mushroom caps, hollows uppermost, on an oiled baking sheet.

3 Put the mushroom stalks, garlic and parsley in a food processor or blender. Process for 1 minute. Turn into a bowl. Add the leek and butter, and season with freshly ground black pepper to taste. Preheat the broiler.

4 Crumble the Stilton into the mushroom mixture, and mix well. Divide the Stilton mixture among the mushroom caps, and broil for 6–7 minutes until bubbling. Serve garnished with frisée lettuce and halved tomatoes, if desired.

Tomato and Okra Stew

Okra is an unusual and delicious vegetable. It releases a sticky sap when cooked, which helps to thicken the stew.

Serves 4

INGREDIENTS
1 tbsp olive oil
1 onion, chopped
12 oz jar pimientos, drained
2 x 14 oz cans chopped tomatoes
10 oz okra
2 tbsp chopped fresh parsley
salt and freshly ground black pepper

parsley

chopped tomatoes

pimientos

onion

okra

1 Heat the oil in a pan. Add the onion, and cook for 2–3 minutes.

2 Coarsely chop the pimientos, and add to the onion. Add the chopped tomatoes, and mix well.

3 Cut the tops off the okra, and cut into halves or quarters if large. Add to the tomato sauce in the pan. Season with plenty of salt and pepper.

4 Bring the vegetable stew to a boil. Then lower the heat, cover the pan, and simmer for 12 minutes until the vegetables are tender and the sauce has thickened. Stir in the chopped parsley, and serve at once.

Vegetable Kebabs with Mustard and Honey

A colorful mixture of vegetables and tofu, skewered, glazed and broiled until tender.

Serves 4

INGREDIENTS
1 yellow bell pepper
2 small zucchini
8 oz piece of firm tofu
8 cherry tomatoes
8 button mushrooms
1 tbsp whole-grain mustard
1 tbsp clear honey
2 tbsp olive oil
salt and freshly ground black pepper

TO SERVE
4 portions cooked mixed rice
 and wild rice
lime segments
flat leaf parsley

1 Cut the pepper in half, and remove the seeds. Cut each half into quarters, and cut each quarter in half.

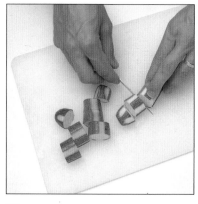

2 Remove the ends from the zucchini and peel them decoratively. Then cut each zucchini into eight chunks.

3 Cut the tofu into pieces of a similar size to the vegetables.

zucchini

cherry tomatoes

yellow bell pepper

clear honey

whole-grain mustard

button mushrooms

tofu

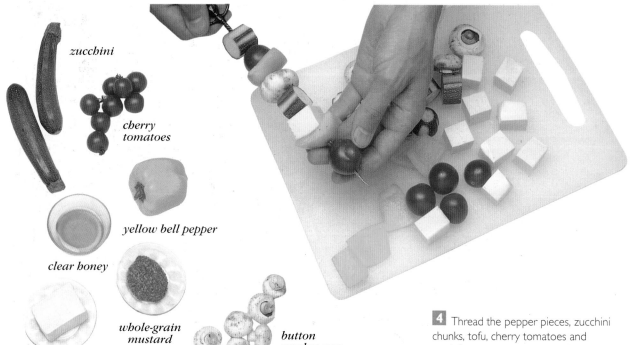

4 Thread the pepper pieces, zucchini chunks, tofu, cherry tomatoes and mushrooms alternately on to four metal or bamboo skewers. Preheat the broiler.

5 Whisk the mustard, honey and olive oil in a small bowl. Add salt and pepper to taste.

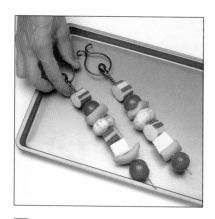

6 Put the kebabs on to a baking sheet. Brush with the mustard and honey glaze. Cook under the broiler for 8 minutes, turning once or twice during cooking. Serve with a mixture of long grain and wild rice, and garnish with lime segments and parsley.

COOK'S TIP
If using bamboo skewers, soak them in a bowl of cold water before threading, to prevent them burning when placed under the broiler.

Deep-fried Florets with Tangy Thyme Mayonnaise

Cauliflower and broccoli make a sensational snack when coated in a beer batter and deep-fried. Serve with a tangy mayonnaise.

Serves 2–3

INGREDIENTS
6 oz cauliflower
6 oz broccoli
2 eggs, separated
2 tbsp olive oil
1 cup beer
1¼ cups all-purpose flour
pinch of salt
2 tbsp shredded fresh basil
vegetable oil for deep-frying
²/₃ cup good quality mayonnaise
2 tsp chopped fresh thyme
2 tsp grated lemon rind
2 tsp lemon juice
sea salt, for sprinkling

eggs
basil
all-purpose flour
mayonnaise
broccoli
cauliflower
beer
thyme
lemon

1 Break the cauliflower and broccoli into small florets, cutting large florets into smaller pieces. Set aside.

2 Beat the egg yolks, olive oil, beer, flour and salt in a bowl. Strain the batter, if necessary, to remove any lumps.

3 Whisk the egg whites until stiff. Fold into the batter with the basil.

4 Heat the oil for deep-frying to 350°F or until a cube of bread, when added to the oil, browns in about 30–45 seconds. Dip the florets in the batter, and deep-fry in batches for 2–3 minutes until the coating is golden and crisp. Drain on paper towels.

5 Mix the mayonnaise, thyme, lemon rind and juice in a small bowl.

6 Sprinkle the florets with sea salt and then serve with the thyme mayonnaise.

Black Bean and Vegetable Stir-fry

The secret of a quick stir-fry is to prepare all the ingredients first. This colorful vegetable mixture is coated in a classic Chinese sauce.

Serves 4

INGREDIENTS
8 scallions
2 cups button mushrooms
1 red bell pepper
1 green bell pepper
2 large carrots
4 tbsp sesame oil
2 garlic cloves, crushed
4 tbsp black bean sauce
6 tbsp warm water
8 oz beansprouts
salt and freshly ground black pepper

1 Thinly slice the scallions and button mushrooms. Set them to one side in separate bowls.

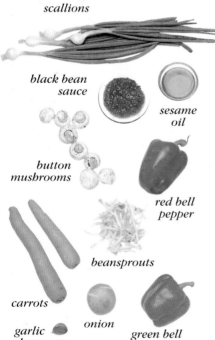

scallions

black bean sauce

sesame oil

button mushrooms

red bell pepper

beansprouts

carrots

garlic cloves

onion

green bell pepper

2 Cut both the bell peppers in half. Remove the seeds, and slice the flesh into thin strips.

3 Cut the carrots in half. Cut each half into thin strips lengthwise. Stack the slices, and cut through them to make very fine strips.

4 Heat the oil in a large wok or frying pan until very hot. Add the scallions and garlic, and stir-fry for 30 seconds.

5 Add the mushrooms, bell peppers and carrots. Stir-fry for 5–6 minutes over a high heat until the vegetables are just beginning to soften.

6 Mix the black bean sauce with the water. Add to the wok or pan, and cook for 3–4 minutes. Stir in the beansprouts, and stir-fry for 1 minute more, until all the vegetables are coated in the sauce. Season to taste. Serve at once.

COOK'S TIP
For best results the oil in the wok must be very hot before adding the vegetables.

French Bread Pizzas with Artichokes

Crunchy French bread makes an ideal base for these quick pizzas.

Serves 4

INGREDIENTS
1 tbsp sunflower oil
1 onion, chopped
1 green bell pepper, seeded and
chopped
7 oz can chopped tomatoes
1 tbsp tomato paste
$\frac{1}{2}$ French stick
14 oz can artichoke hearts, drained
4 oz mozzarella cheese, sliced
1 tbsp poppy seeds
salt and freshly ground black pepper

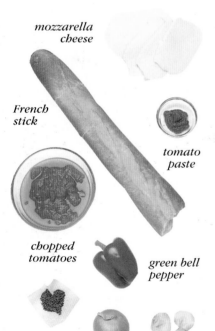

mozzarella cheese

French stick

tomato paste

chopped tomatoes

green bell pepper

poppy seeds

onion

artichoke hearts

1 Heat the oil in a frying pan. Add the chopped onion and bell pepper, and cook for 4 minutes until just softened.

2 Stir in the chopped tomatoes and tomato paste. Cook for 4 minutes. Remove from the heat, and add salt and pepper to taste.

3 Cut the piece of French stick in half lengthwise. Cut each half in four to give eight pieces in all.

4 Spoon a little of the pepper and tomato mixture over each piece of bread. Preheat the broiler.

5 Slice the artichoke hearts. Arrange them on top of the pepper and tomato mixture. Cover with the mozzarella slices, and sprinkle with the poppy seeds.

6 Arrange the French bread pizzas on a rack over a broiler pan, and broil for 6–8 minutes until the cheese melts and is beginning to brown. Serve at once.

New Spring Salad

This chunky salad makes a satisfying meal. Use other spring vegetables, if you like.

Serves 4

INGREDIENTS

1½ lb small new potatoes, halved
14 oz can fava beans, drained
4 oz cherry tomatoes
½ cup walnut halves
2 tbsp white wine vinegar
1 tbsp whole-grain mustard
4 tbsp olive oil
pinch of sugar
8 oz young asparagus spears,
    trimmed
6 scallions, trimmed
salt and freshly ground black pepper
baby spinach leaves, to serve

asparagus spears

new potatoes

whole-grain mustard

fava beans

cherry tomatoes

scallions

walnut halves

1 Put the potatoes in a pan. Cover with cold water, and bring to a boil. Cook for 10–12 minutes, until tender. Meanwhile, turn the fava beans into a bowl. Cut the tomatoes in half, and add them to the bowl with the walnuts.

2 Put the white wine vinegar, mustard, olive oil and sugar into a jar. Add salt and pepper to taste. Close the jar tightly, and shake well.

3 Add the asparagus to the potatoes, and cook for 3 minutes more. Drain the cooked vegetables well. Cool under cold running water, and drain again. Thickly slice the potatoes, and cut the scallions into halves.

4 Add the asparagus, potatoes and scallions to the bowl containing the fava bean mixture. Pour the dressing over the salad, and toss well. Serve on a bed of baby spinach leaves.

Brioche with Mixed Mushrooms

Mushrooms in a rich sherry sauce, served on toasted brioche, make a delectable, light lunch, but would also serve 6 as an appetizer.

Serves 4

INGREDIENTS
6 tbsp butter
1 vegetable bouillon cube
1½ lb shiitake mushrooms, caps only, sliced
8 oz button mushrooms, sliced
3 tbsp dry sherry
1 cup sour cream
2 tsp lemon juice
4 thick slices of brioche
salt and freshly ground black pepper

shiitake and button mushrooms   *brioche*

butter

bouillon cube   *sour cream*

lemon

COOK'S TIP
If shiitake mushrooms are too expensive or not available, substitute more button or crimini mushrooms. Always wipe the mushrooms with paper towels before use.

1 Melt the butter in a large pan. Crumble in the bouillon cube, and stir for about 30 seconds.

2 Add the shiitake and button mushrooms to the pan, and cook for 5 minutes over a moderate to high heat, stirring occasionally.

3 Stir in the sherry. Cook for 1 minute, then add the sour cream. Cook, stirring, over a gentle heat for 5 minutes. Stir in the lemon juice, and add salt and pepper to taste. Preheat the broiler.

4 Toast the brioche slices under the broiler until just golden on both sides. Spoon the mushrooms on top, heat briefly under the broiler, and serve. Fresh thyme may be used to garnish, if desired.

Ratatouille with Camembert Croûtons

Crisp croûtons and creamy Camembert provide a tasty topping on hot ratatouille. Either buy the ratatouille at a deli counter or make your own.

Serves 2

INGREDIENTS
3 thick slices of white bread
8 oz firm Camembert cheese
4 tbsp olive oil
1 garlic clove, chopped
3/4–1 lb ratatouille
parsley sprigs, to garnish

ratatouille

parsley

garlic clove

Camembert cheese

white bread

1 Trim the crusts from the bread slices, and discard. Cut the bread and the Camembert into 1 in squares.

2 Heat 3 tbsp of the oil in a frying pan. Add the bread, and cook over a high heat for 5 minutes, stirring constantly, until golden all over. Reduce the heat, add the garlic, and cook for 1 minute more. Remove the croûtons with a slotted spoon.

3 Turn the ratatouille into a pan, and place over a medium heat, stirring occasionally, until hot.

4 Heat the remaining oil in the frying pan. Add the cheese cubes, and sear over a high heat for 1 minute. Divide the hot ratatouille between two serving bowls. Spoon the croûtons and cheese on top, garnish with the parsley, and serve at once.

Crusty Rolls with Zucchini and Saffron

Split, crusty rolls are filled with zucchini in a creamy tomato sauce flavored with saffron. Use a mixture of green zucchini and yellow summer squash, if possible.

Serves 4

INGREDIENTS

1½ lb small zucchini
1 tbsp olive oil
2 shallots, finely chopped
4 crusty rolls
7 oz can chopped tomatoes
pinch of sugar
a few saffron threads
¼ cup light cream
salt and freshly ground black pepper

zucchini

chopped tomatoes

saffron

shallots

crusty rolls   *light cream*

1 Preheat the oven to 350°F. Remove the ends from the zucchini, then, using a sharp knife, cut the zucchini into 1½ in lengths. Cut each piece into quarters lengthwise.

COOK'S TIP

To avoid heating your oven, heat the rolls in a microwave. Put them on a plate, cover with paper towels, and heat on HIGH for 30–45 seconds.

2 Heat the oil in a large frying pan. Add the shallots, and fry over moderate heat for 1–2 minutes. Put the rolls into the oven to warm through.

3 Add the zucchini to the shallots. Mix well, and cook for 6 minutes, stirring frequently, until just beginning to soften.

4 Stir in the tomatoes and sugar. Steep the saffron threads in a little hot water for a few minutes, then add to the pan with the cream. Cook for 4 minutes, stirring occasionally. Season to taste. Split open the rolls, and fill with the zucchini and sauce.

Cheese en Croûte with Tomato Sauce

Melt-in-the-mouth cheese sandwiches, pan-fried and served with a tomato sauce.

Serves 4

INGREDIENTS
1/4 cup butter, softened
1 small onion, chopped
14 oz can chopped tomatoes
large thyme sprig
8 slices of white bread
4 oz aged Cheddar cheese
2 eggs
2 tbsp milk
2 tbsp peanut oil
salt and freshly ground black pepper
8 Romaine lettuce leaves, to serve

thyme

eggs

chopped tomatoes

onion

milk

Cheddar cheese

butter

white bread

1 Melt 2 tbsp of the butter in a frying pan. Add the onion, and cook for 3–4 minutes until soft.

2 Stir in the chopped tomatoes. Strip the leaves from the thyme sprig, and stir them into the pan. Add salt and pepper to taste. Then cover the pan, and cook for 5 minutes.

3 Meanwhile, spread the remaining butter over the slices of bread.

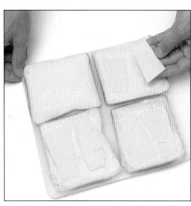

4 Slice the cheese thinly. Arrange on four slices of bread, and sandwich with the remaining slices. Trim the crusts.

5 Beat the eggs and milk together in a bowl. Add salt and pepper to taste, and pour into a shallow dish.

6 Heat the oil in a large frying pan. Dip each sandwich in the egg mixture until well-coated. Add to the hot oil, and fry for 2 minutes on each side, until the coating is golden and the cheese has melted. Cut each sandwich into quarters. Arrange on individual plates garnished with the Romaine lettuce leaves. Serve the tomato sauce in a bowl to one side.

COOK'S TIP
If the tomato sauce is a little tart, add a pinch of sugar, or liven it up with a dash of Tabasco.

Potato, Broccoli and Red Bell Pepper Stir-fry

A hot and hearty stir-fry of vegetables with just a hint of fresh ginger.

Serves 2

INGREDIENTS
1 lb potatoes
3 tbsp peanut oil
¼ cup butter
1 small onion, chopped
1 red bell pepper, seeded and
  chopped
8 oz broccoli, broken into florets
1 in piece of fresh ginger, peeled
  and grated
salt and freshly ground black pepper

red bell pepper   *butter*

broccoli   *onion*

fresh ginger   *potatoes*

1 Peel the potatoes, and cut them into ½ in dice.

2 Heat the oil in a large frying pan, and add the potatoes. Cook for 8 minutes over a high heat, stirring and tossing occasionally, until the potatoes are browned and just tender.

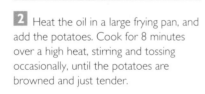

3 Drain off the oil. Add the butter to the potatoes in the pan. As soon as it melts, add the onion and red bell pepper. Stir-fry for 2 minutes.

4 Add the broccoli florets and ginger to the pan. Stir-fry for 2–3 minutes more, taking care not to break up the potatoes. Add salt and pepper to taste, and serve at once.

COOK'S TIP

Although a wok is the preferred pan for stir-frying, for this recipe, a flat frying pan is best to cook the potatoes quickly.

78

Bubble and Squeak with Fried Eggs

Originally made with meat and cabbage in England centuries ago, this dish was named for its noisy cooking.

Serves 2

INGREDIENTS
½ Savoy cabbage
¼ cup butter
1 small onion, finely chopped
1 lb mashed potato
1 tbsp chopped fresh parsley
1 tbsp vegetable oil
2 eggs
salt and freshly ground black pepper
2 tomatoes, halved, to serve

eggs

mashed potato

butter

onion

Savoy cabbage

parsley

1 Cut out and discard the hard core of the cabbage. Strip off and discard the outer layer of leaves. Finely slice the remaining cabbage, and set aside.

2 Melt the butter in a large frying pan. Add the onion, and fry for 2–3 minutes until just tender. Reduce the heat slightly. Add the cabbage, and cook, stirring constantly, for 2–3 minutes.

3 Add the mashed potato to the pan. Stir to combine. Cook for 5–6 minutes until the mixture starts to brown. Stir in the chopped parsley, and add salt and pepper to taste. Transfer the mixture to a serving dish, and keep hot.

4 Wipe the pan clean. Heat the oil, and fry the eggs until just set. Serve the bubble and squeak on individual plates, adding a fried egg and two tomato halves to each portion. Sprinkle with black pepper.

Potato, Spinach and Pine Nut Gratin

Pine nuts add a satisfying crunch to this gratin of wafer-thin potato slices and spinach in a creamy cheese sauce.

Serves 2

INGREDIENTS
1 lb potatoes
1 garlic clove, crushed
3 scallions, thinly sliced
²/₃ cup light cream
1 cup milk
8 oz frozen chopped spinach, thawed
4 oz Cheddar cheese, grated
¹/₄ cup pine nuts
salt and freshly ground black pepper

spinach

potatoes

garlic clove

pine nuts

scallions

Cheddar cheese

light cream

1 Peel the potatoes, and cut them carefully into wafer-thin slices. Spread them out in a large, heavy-bottomed, nonstick frying pan.

2 Sprinkle the crushed garlic and sliced scallions evenly over the potatoes.

3 Pour the cream and milk over the potatoes. Place the pan over a gentle heat. Cover, and cook for 8 minutes or until the potatoes are tender.

4 Using both hands, squeeze the spinach dry. Add the spinach to the potatoes, mixing lightly. Cover the pan, and cook for 2 minutes more.

5 Add salt and pepper to taste, then spoon the mixture into a shallow casserole. Preheat the broiler.

6 Sprinkle the grated cheese and pine nuts over the spinach mixture. Heat under the broiler for 2–3 minutes until the topping is golden. A simple lettuce and tomato salad makes an excellent accompaniment to this dish.

Creamy Cannellini Beans with Asparagus

Cannellini beans in a creamy sauce contrast with tender asparagus in this tasty toast topper.

Serves 2

INGREDIENTS
2 tsp butter
1 small onion, finely chopped
1 small carrot, grated
1 tsp fresh thyme leaves
14 oz can cannellini beans, drained
²/₃ cup light cream
4 oz young asparagus spears, trimmed
2 slices of fresh sliced whole wheat bread
salt and freshly ground black pepper

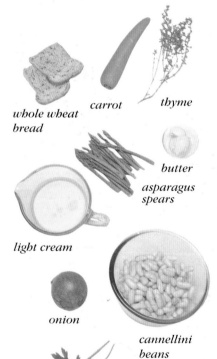

whole wheat bread

carrot

thyme

butter

asparagus spears

light cream

onion

cannellini beans

parsley

1 Melt the butter in a pan. Add the onion and carrot, and fry over a moderate heat for 4 minutes until soft. Add the thyme leaves.

2 Rinse the cannellini beans under cold running water. Drain thoroughly. Then add to the onion and carrot. Mix lightly.

3 Pour in the cream, and heat slowly to just below boiling point, stirring occasionally. Remove the pan from the heat, and add salt and pepper to taste. Preheat the broiler.

4 Place the asparagus spears in a saucepan. Pour over just enough boiling water to cover. Poach for 3–4 minutes until the spears are just tender.

5 Meanwhile, toast the bread under the broiler until both sides are golden.

6 Place the toast on individual plates. Drain the asparagus, and divide the spears between the slices of toast. Spoon the bean mixture over each portion, and serve.

Red Fried Rice

This vibrant rice dish owes its appeal as much to the bright colors of red onion, red bell pepper and tomatoes as it does to their flavors.

Serves 2

INGREDIENTS
¾ cup basmati rice
2 tbsp peanut oil
1 small red onion, chopped
1 red bell pepper, seeded and
  chopped
8 oz cherry tomatoes, halved
2 eggs, beaten
salt and freshly ground black pepper

eggs

basmati rice

cherry tomatoes

red onion

red bell pepper

1 Wash the rice several times under cold running water. Drain well. Bring a large pan of water to a boil. Add the rice, and cook for 10–12 minutes.

2 Meanwhile, heat the oil in a wok until very hot. Add the onion and red pepper, and stir-fry for 2–3 minutes. Add the cherry tomatoes, and stir-fry for 2 minutes more.

3 Pour in the beaten eggs all at once. Cook for 30 seconds without stirring, then stir to break up the egg as it sets.

4 Drain the cooked rice thoroughly. Add to the wok, and toss it over the heat with the vegetable and egg mixture for 3 minutes. Season the fried rice with salt and pepper to taste.

Chick-pea Stew

This hearty chick-pea and vegetable stew makes a filling meal. It is delicious served with garlic-flavored mashed potatoes.

Serves 4

INGREDIENTS

2 tbsp olive oil
1 small onion, chopped
8 oz carrots, halved lengthwise
  and thinly sliced
$\frac{1}{2}$ tsp ground cumin
1 tsp ground coriander
2 tbsp all-purpose flour
8 oz zucchini, sliced
7 oz can corn, drained
14 oz can chick-peas, drained
2 tbsp tomato paste
scant 1 cup hot vegetable bouillon,
  made from a cube
salt and freshly ground black pepper

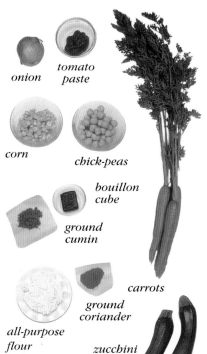

onion   tomato paste

corn   chick-peas

bouillon cube

ground cumin

all-purpose flour

carrots

ground coriander

zucchini

1 Heat the oil in a frying pan. Add the onion and carrots. Toss to coat the vegetables in the oil. Then cook over moderate heat for 4 minutes.

2 Add the ground cumin, coriander and flour. Stir, and cook for 1 minute.

COOK'S TIP

For speedy garlic-flavored mashed potatoes, simply mash potatoes with garlic butter and stir in chopped fresh parsley and a little sour cream.

3 Cut the zucchini slices in half., then add them to the pan with the corn, chick-peas, tomato paste and vegetable bouillon. Stir well. Cook gently for 10 minutes, stirring frequently.

4 Taste the stew, and add salt and pepper. Serve at once, with garlic-flavored mashed potatoes (see Cook's Tip), if desired.

Eggplant Pilaf

This hearty dish is made with bulgur and eggplant, flavored with fresh mint.

Serves 2

INGREDIENTS

2 eggplants
4–6 tbsp sunflower oil
1 small onion, finely chopped
1 cup bulgur
scant 2 cups vegetable bouillon,
  made from a cube
2 tbsp pine nuts, toasted
1 tbsp chopped fresh mint
salt and freshly ground black pepper

FOR THE GARNISH
lime wedges
lemon wedges
torn mint leaves

COOK'S TIP

To cut down on the cooking time, soak the bulgur in water to cover by 1 in for up to 8 hours. Drain, and then continue as described in the recipe below, reducing the cooking time to just 8 minutes.

1 Remove the ends from the eggplants. Using a sharp knife, cut them into neat sticks and then into ½ in dice.

2 Heat 4 tbsp of the oil in a large frying pan. Add the onion, and sauté for 1 minute.

3 Add the diced eggplants. Cook over a high heat, stirring frequently, for about 4 minutes until just tender. Add the remaining oil, if needed.

4 Stir in the bulgur, mixing well. Then pour in the vegetable bouillon. Bring to a boil. Then lower the heat, and simmer for 10 minutes or until all the liquid has evaporated. Season to taste.

5 Add the pine nuts, and stir gently with a wooden spoon. Stir in the mint.

6 Spoon the pilaf on to individual plates, and garnish each portion with lime and lemon wedges. Sprinkle with torn mint leaves for extra color.

Hummus with Pan-fried Zucchini

Pan-fried zucchini are perfect for dipping into homemade hummus.

Serves 4

INGREDIENTS
8 oz can chick-peas
2 garlic cloves, coarsely chopped
6 tbsp lemon juice
4 tbsp tahini
5 tbsp olive oil, plus extra to serve
1 tsp ground cumin
1 lb small zucchini
salt and freshly ground black pepper

TO SERVE
paprika
pita bread
black olives

zucchini

chick peas

lemon

tahini

garlic cloves

ground cumin

1 Drain the chick-peas, reserving the liquid from the can, and turn them into a food processor or blender. Blend to a smooth paste, adding a small amount of the reserved liquid, if necessary.

2 Mix the garlic, lemon juice and tahini together, and add to the food processor or blender. Process until smooth. With the machine running, gradually add 3 tbsp of the olive oil through the feeder tube or lid.

3 Add the cumin, with salt and pepper to taste. Process to mix. Then scrape the hummus into a bowl. Cover, and chill until required.

4 Remove the ends from the zucchini. Slice the zucchini lengthwise into even-size pieces.

5 Heat the remaining oil in a large frying pan. Season the zucchini, and fry them for 2–3 minutes on each side until just tender.

COOK'S TIP
Hummus is also delicious served with pan-fried or broiled eggplant slices.

6 Divide the zucchini among four individual plates. Spoon a portion of hummus on to each plate, and sprinkle with paprika. Add two or three pieces of sliced pita bread, and serve with olives.

Lentil Stir-fry

Mushrooms, artichokes, sugar snap peas and lentils make a satisfying stir-fry supper.

Serves 2–3

INGREDIENTS

4 oz sugar snap peas
1 oz butter
1 small onion, chopped
4 oz cup or button mushrooms, sliced
14 oz can artichoke hearts, drained and halved
14 oz can green lentils, drained
4 tbsp light cream
¼ cup shaved almonds, toasted
salt and freshly ground black pepper
French bread, to serve

light cream   *green lentils*

cup mushrooms   *sugar snap peas*

shaved almonds   *artichoke hearts*

onion

COOK'S TIP
Use strained, plain yogurt instead of the cream, if you like.

1 Bring a pan of salted water to a boil. Add the sugar snap peas, and cook for about 4 minutes until just tender. Drain, and refresh under cold running water. Then drain again. Pat dry the peas with paper towels, and set aside.

2 Melt the butter in a frying pan. Add the chopped onion and cook for 2–3 minutes, stirring occasionally.

3 Add the sliced mushrooms to the onion. Stir until combined. Then cook for 2–3 minutes until just tender. Add the artichokes, sugar snap peas and lentils to the pan. Stir-fry for 2 minutes.

4 Stir in the cream and almonds, and cook for 1 minute. Season to taste. Serve at once, with chunks of French bread.

Nut Pilaf with Omelet Rolls

A wonderful mixture of textures – soft, fluffy rice with crunchy nuts and omelet rolls.

Serves 2

INGREDIENTS

1 cup basmati rice
1 tbsp sunflower oil
1 small onion, chopped
1 red bell pepper, finely diced
1½ cups hot vegetable bouillon,
  made from a cube
2 eggs
¼ cup salted peanuts
1 tbsp soy sauce
salt and freshly ground black pepper
parsley sprigs, to garnish

salted peanuts   *parsley*   *onion*

bouillon cube

eggs

red bell pepper

basmati rice

1 Wash the rice several times under cold running water. Drain thoroughly. Heat half the oil in a large frying pan. Fry the onion and bell pepper for 2–3 minutes. Then stir in the rice and bouillon. Bring to a boil, and cook for 10 minutes until the rice is tender.

2 Meanwhile, beat the eggs lightly with salt and pepper to taste. Heat the remaining oil in a second large frying pan. Pour in the eggs, and tilt the pan to cover the base thinly. Cook the omelet for 1 minute. Then flip it over, and cook the other side for 1 minute.

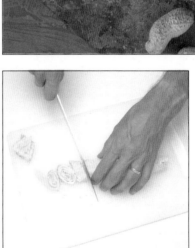

3 Carefully slide the omelet on to a clean board, and roll it up tightly. Cut the omelet roll into eight slices.

4 Stir the peanuts and soy sauce into the pilaf, and add black pepper to taste. Turn the pilaf into a serving dish. Arrange the omelet rolls on top, and garnish with the parsley. Serve at once.

Kedgeree with Green Beans and Mushrooms

Crunchy green beans and mushrooms are the star ingredients in this vegetarian version of an old favorite.

Serves 2

INGREDIENTS
³/₄ cup basmati rice
1¹/₄ cups cold water
3 eggs
6 oz green beans, trimmed
¹/₄ cup butter
1 onion, finely chopped
8 oz crimini mushrooms, quartered
2 tbsp light cream
1 tbsp chopped fresh parsley
salt and freshly ground black pepper

light cream   *crimini mushrooms*   *parsley*

onion

butter

green beans

eggs

basmati rice

1 Wash the rice several times under cold running water. Drain thoroughly. Bring a pan of water to a boil. Add the rice, and cook for 10–12 minutes until tender. Drain thoroughly.

2 Half fill a second pan with water. Add the eggs, and bring to a boil. Lower the heat, and simmer for 8 minutes. Drain the eggs, and cool them under cold water. Remove the shells.

3 Bring another pan of water to a boil, and cook the green beans for 5 minutes. Drain, and refresh under cold running water. Then drain again.

4 Melt the butter in a large frying pan. Add the onions and mushrooms. Cook for 2–3 minutes over a moderate heat.

5 Add the green beans and rice to the onion mixture. Stir lightly to mix. Cook for 2 minutes. Cut the hard-boiled eggs in wedges, and add them to the pan.

6 Stir in the cream and parsley, taking care not to break up the eggs. Reheat the kedgeree, but do not allow it to boil. Serve at once.

Chick-pea Falafel with Cilantro Dip

Little balls of spicy chick-pea purée, deep-fried until crisp, are served together with a cilantro-flavored mayonnaise.

Serves 4

INGREDIENTS
14 oz can chick-peas, drained
6 scallions, finely sliced
1 egg
½ tsp ground turmeric
1 garlic clove, crushed
1 tsp ground cumin
4 tbsp chopped fresh cilantro
oil for deep-frying
1 small red chili, seeded and
  finely chopped
3 tbsp mayonnaise
salt and freshly ground black pepper
cilantro sprig, to garnish

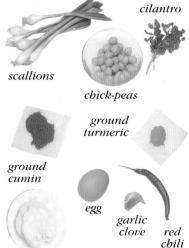

cilantro

scallions

chick-peas

ground turmeric

ground cumin

egg

garlic clove

red chili

mayonnaise

COOK'S TIP
If you have time, chill the chick-pea purée before making it into balls. It will be easier to shape.

1 Turn the chick-peas into a food processor or blender. Add the scallions, and process to a smooth purée. Add the egg, ground turmeric, garlic, cumin and about 1 tbsp of the chopped cilantro. Process briefly to mix, then add salt and pepper to taste.

2 Working with clean, wet hands, shape the chick-pea mixture into about sixteen small balls.

3 Heat the oil for deep-frying to 350°F or until a cube of bread, when added to the oil, browns in 30–45 seconds. Deep-fry the falafel in batches for 2–3 minutes or until golden. Drain on paper towels. Then place in a serving bowl.

4 Stir the remaining cilantro and the chili into the mayonnaise. Garnish with the cilantro sprig, and serve alongside the falafel.

Three Bean Salad with Yogurt Dressing

This tangy bean and pasta salad is great on its own or can be served as a side dish.

Serves 3–4

INGREDIENTS

3 oz penne or other dried
  pasta shapes
2 tomatoes
7 oz canned red kidney beans,
  drained
7 oz canned cannellini beans,
  drained
7 oz canned chick-peas, drained
1 green bell pepper, seeded and
  diced
3 tbsp plain yogurt
2 tbsp sunflower oil
grated rind of ½ lemon
2 tsp whole-grain mustard
1 tsp chopped fresh oregano
salt and freshly ground black pepper

oregano
penne
green bell pepper
red kidney beans
cannellini beans
plain yogurt
chick-peas
lemon
whole-grain mustard
tomatoes

1 Bring a large pan of salted water to a boil. Add the pasta, and cook for 10–12 minutes until just tender. Drain. Cool under cold water, and drain again.

2 Make a cross with the tip of a sharp knife in each of the tomatoes. Plunge them into a bowl of boiling water for 30 seconds. Remove with a slotted spoon or spatula, run under cold water, and peel away the skins. Cut the tomatoes into segments.

3 Drain the canned beans and chick-peas in a colander. Rinse them under cold water, and drain again. Turn into a bowl. Add the tomato segments, green bell pepper and pasta.

4 Whisk the yogurt until smooth. Gradually whisk in the oil, lemon rind and mustard. Stir in the oregano and salt and pepper to taste. Pour the dressing over the salad, and toss well.

INDEX